Peyo

a SMURF adventure

King Smurf

Written by Y. DELPORTE and PEYO

Random House 🏠 New York

THE CAMPAIGN IS NOW IN FULL SWING...

VOTE SMURF

ALL FOR SMURF

I LIKE SMURF

Vote SMURF

BLINK BLONK

VOTE FOR SMURF

BLINK BLONK

FOR A BETTER SMURF, VOTE SMURF

TONIGHT CAMPAIGN SPEECH BY THE ONE AND ONLY SMURF SMURF ONE, SMURF ALL!

HERE HE IS!

CLAP CLAP CLAP CLAP

VOTE SMURF

VOTE SMURF

AND THEN, PAPA SMURF SAID, "SMURF SOFTLY AND CARRY A BIG SMURF," AND I'VE ALWAYS SMURFED THE SAME THING, BECAUSE IF YOU WANT TO SMURF THE NAIL ON THE HEAD AND SMURF DOWN TO BRASS SMURFS...

SHH!

FELLOW SMURFS!

I'D LIKE TO BEGIN BY MAKING ONE THING PERFECTLY SMURF. WE HAVE ONLY ONE THING TO SMURF AND THAT SMURF IS SMURF ITSELF, BUT OUR SMURFS WILL NEVER SMURF ON FOREIGN SMURF, SO ASK NOT WHAT YOUR COUNTRY CAN SMURF FOR YOU BUT RATHER WHAT YOU CAN SMURF FOR YOUR SMURF.

... FOR ALL SMURFS WERE CREATED EQUAL AND ARE ENTITLED TO SMURF, LIBERTY AND THE PURSUIT OF SMURFNESS, SO THE GOVERNMENT OF THE SMURFS, BY THE SMURFS, FOR THE SMURFS SHALL NOT SMURF FROM THIS SMURF! A VOTE FOR ME IS A VOTE FOR SMURF!

HEAR! HEAR! THAT'S SMURFING 'EM!

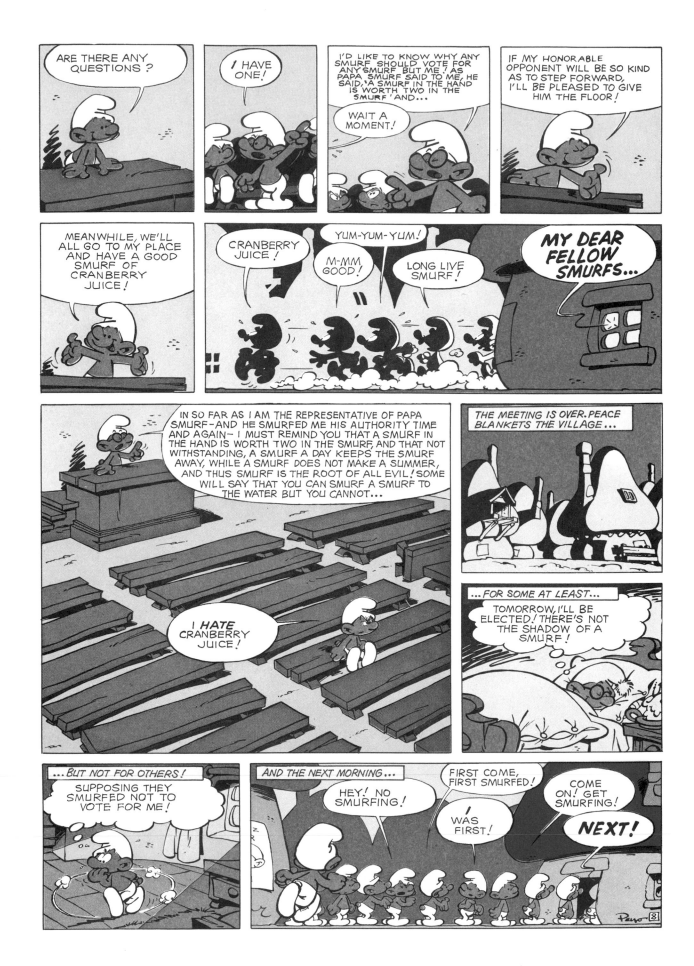

NIGHT HAS SMURFED...

CLOMP CLOMP CLOMP

WHEW! *THAT* WAS A CLOSE SMURF!

KNOCK KNOCK KNOCK KNOCK -KNOCK BANG

WHY DID THE SMURF SMURF THE ROAD?

TO SMURF TO THE OTHER SMURF!

OK, COME IN!

EVERYBODY'S HERE. WE CAN SMURF THE MEETING!

18

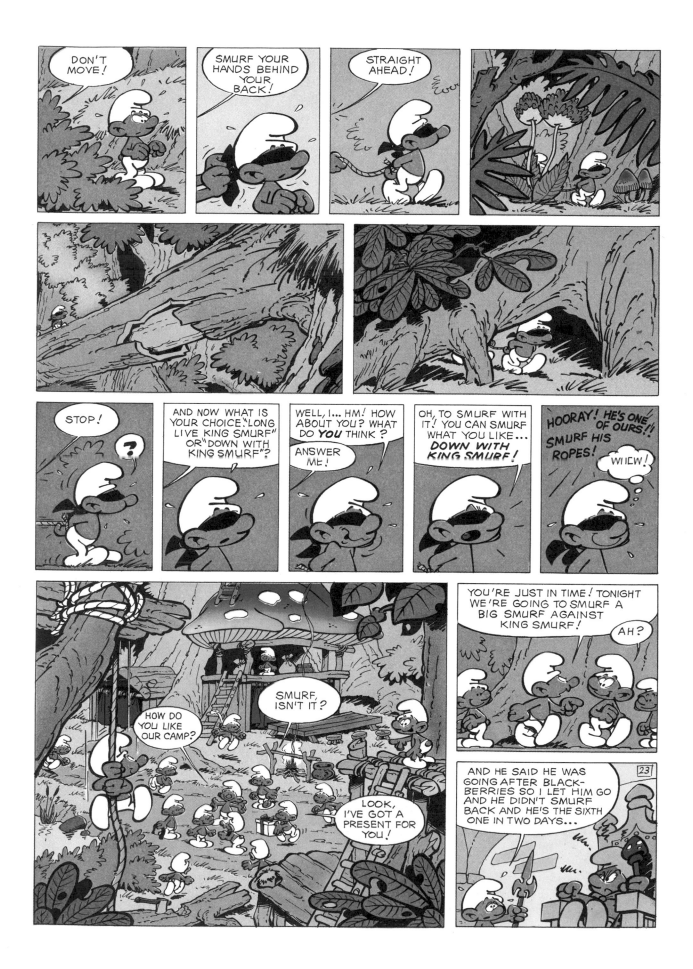

33

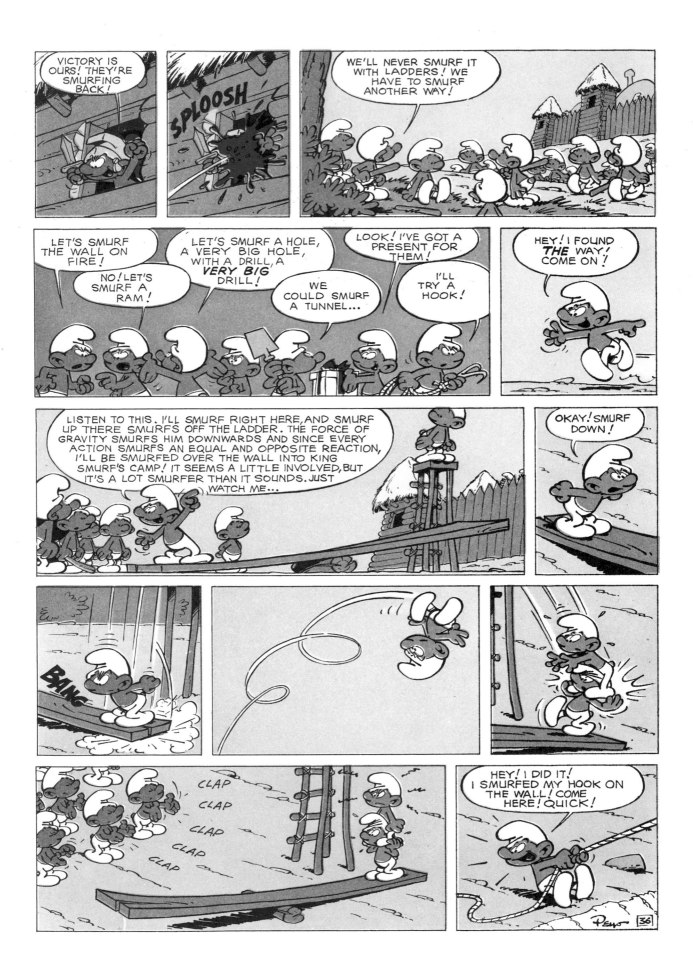

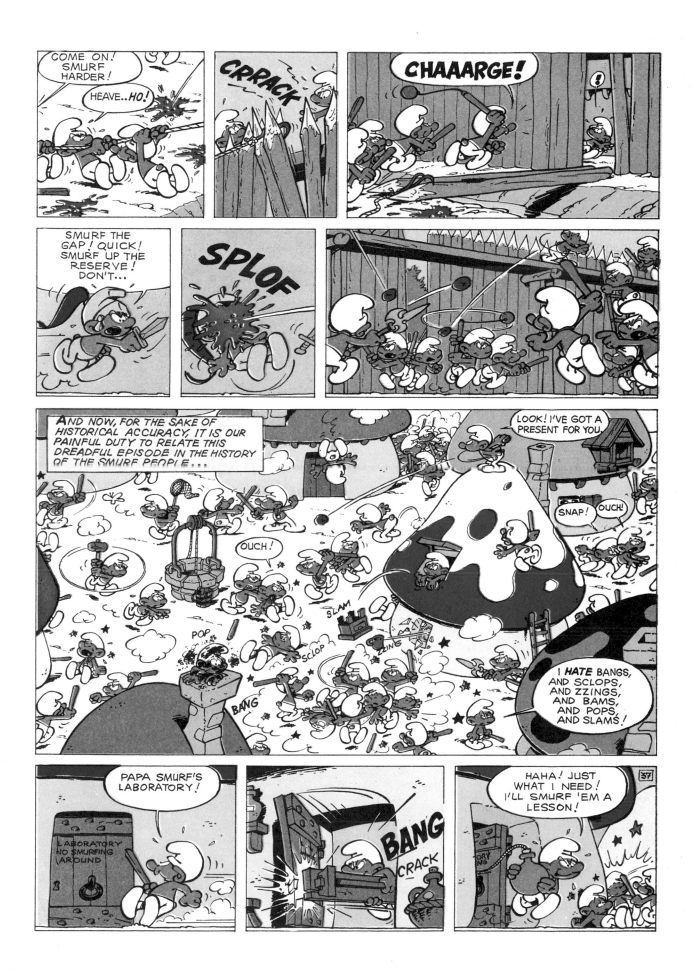

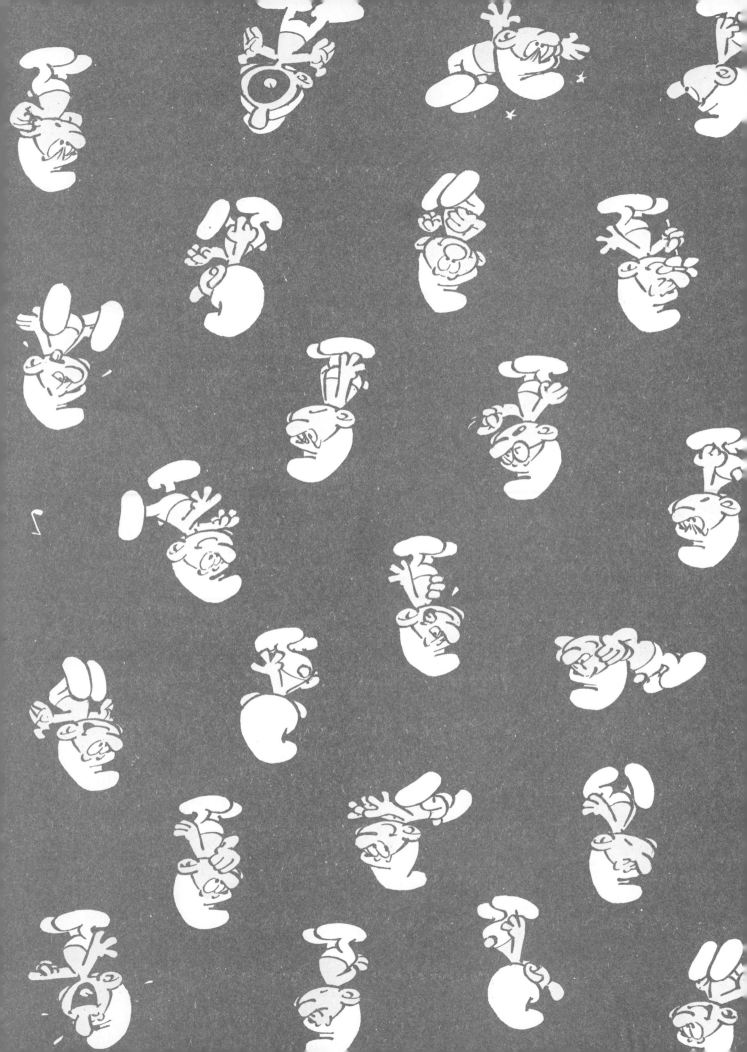

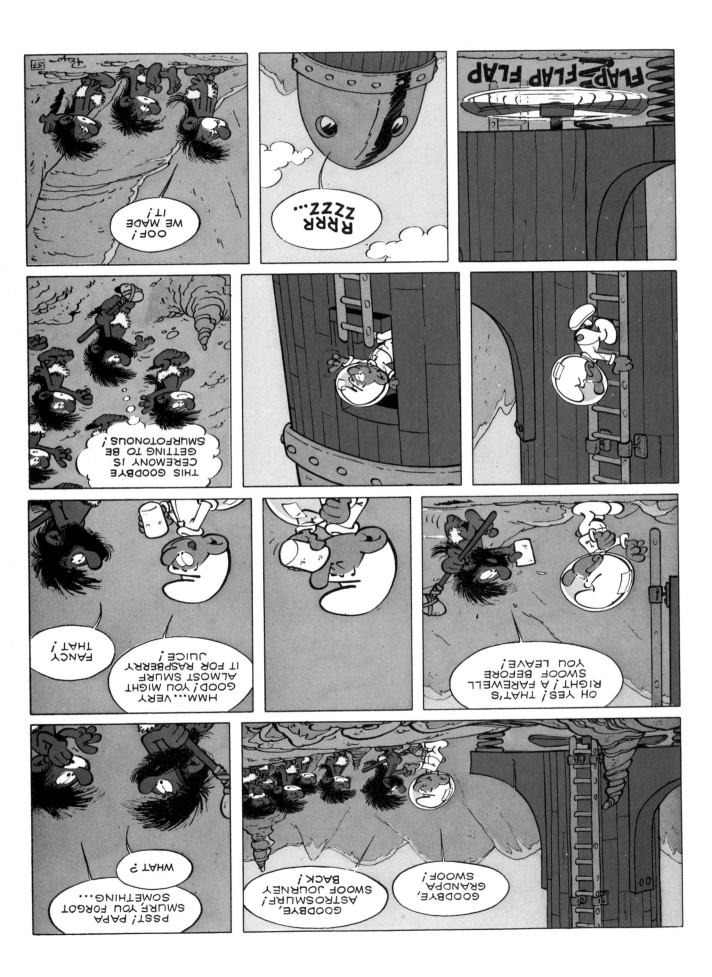

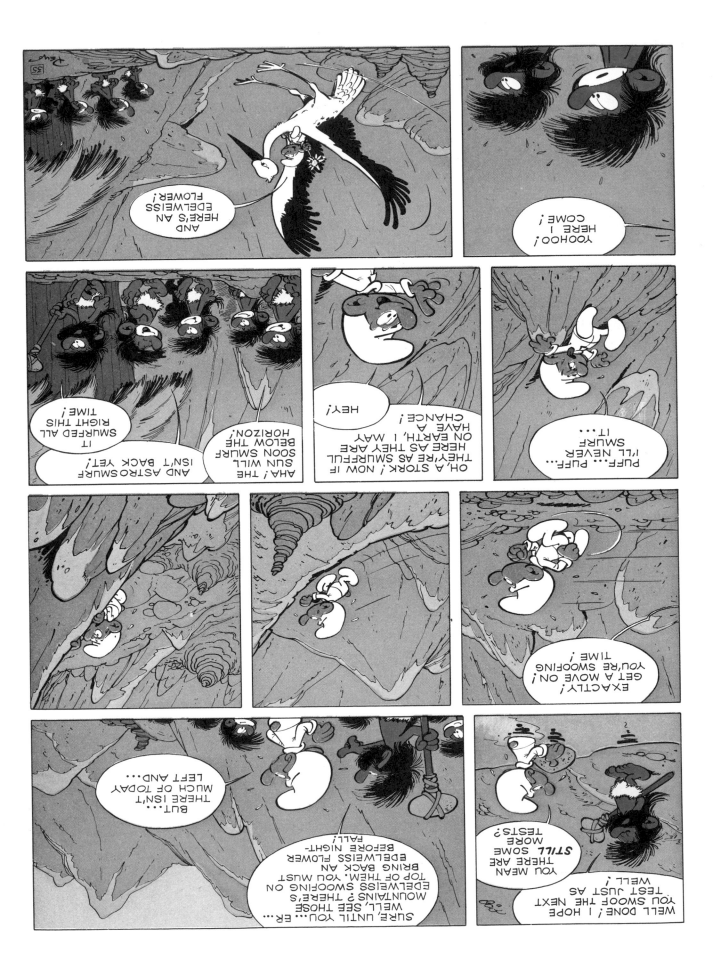

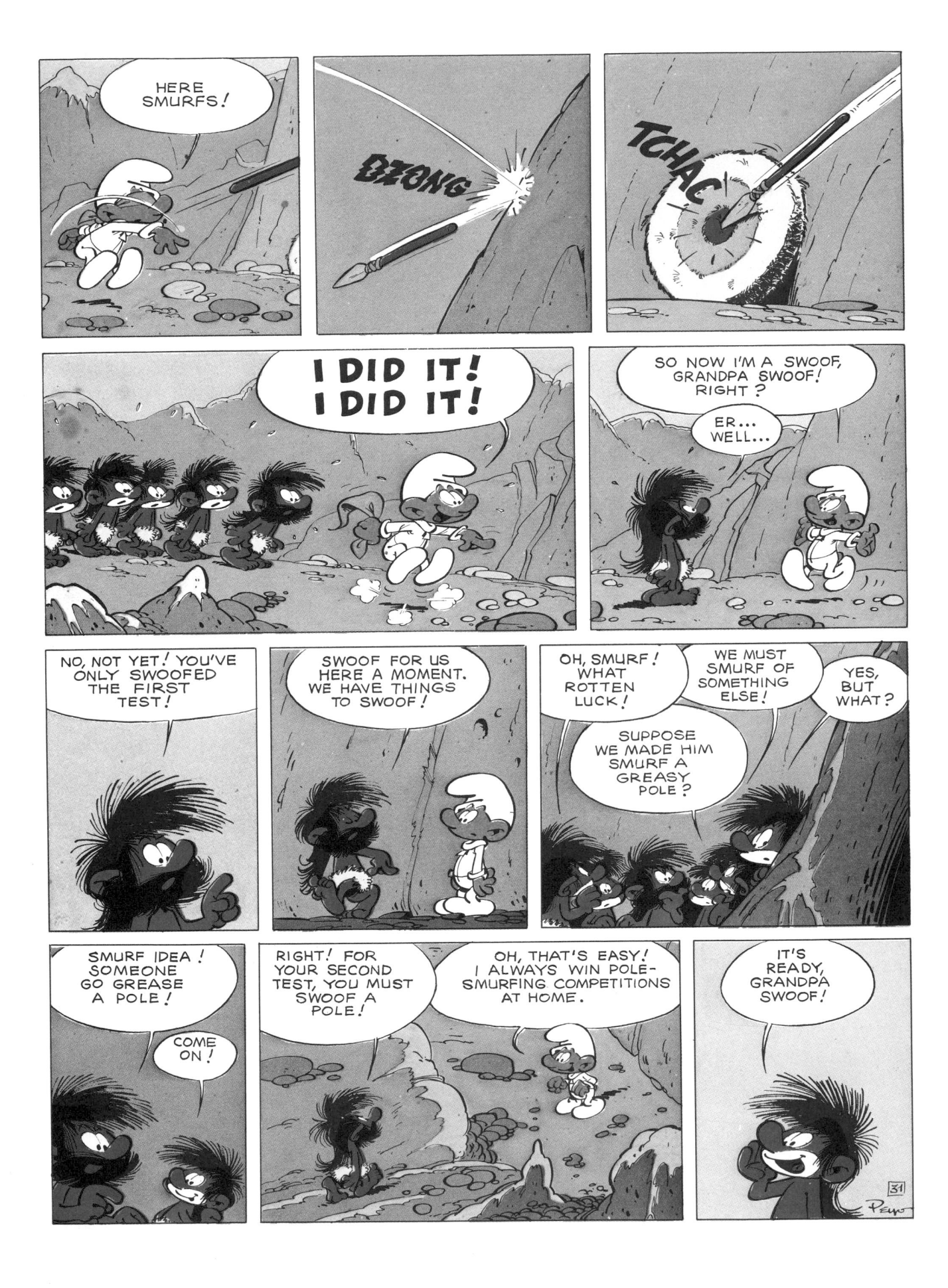

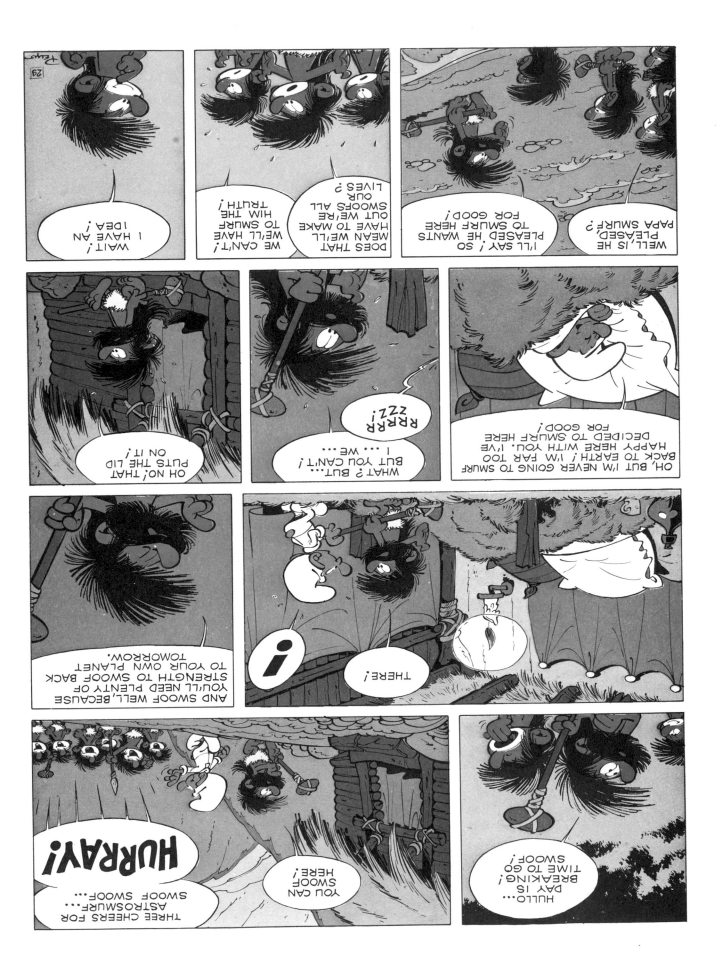

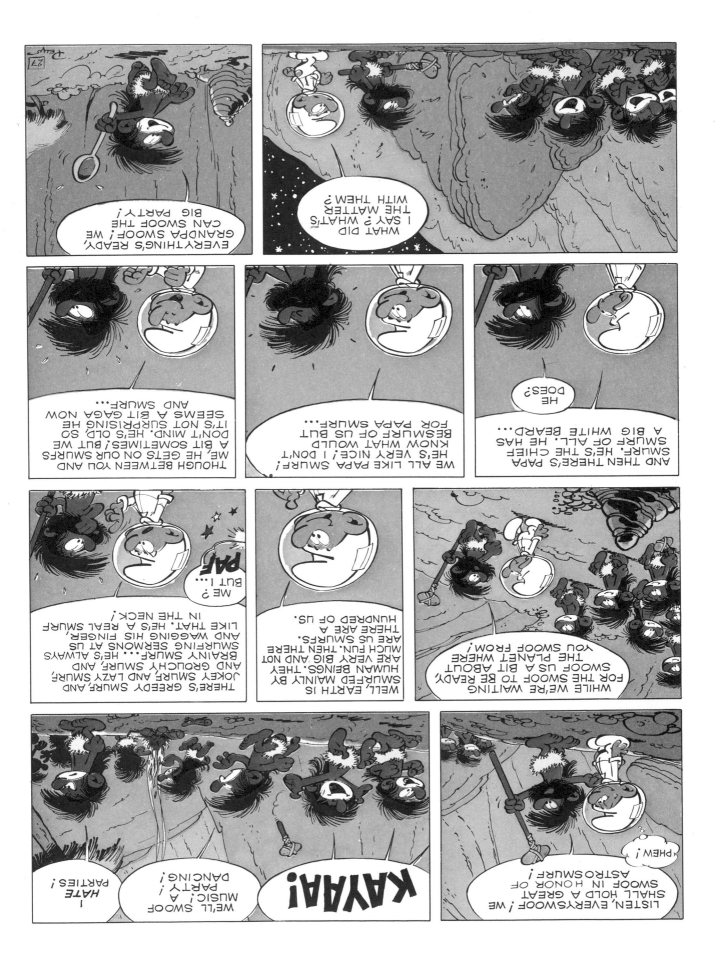

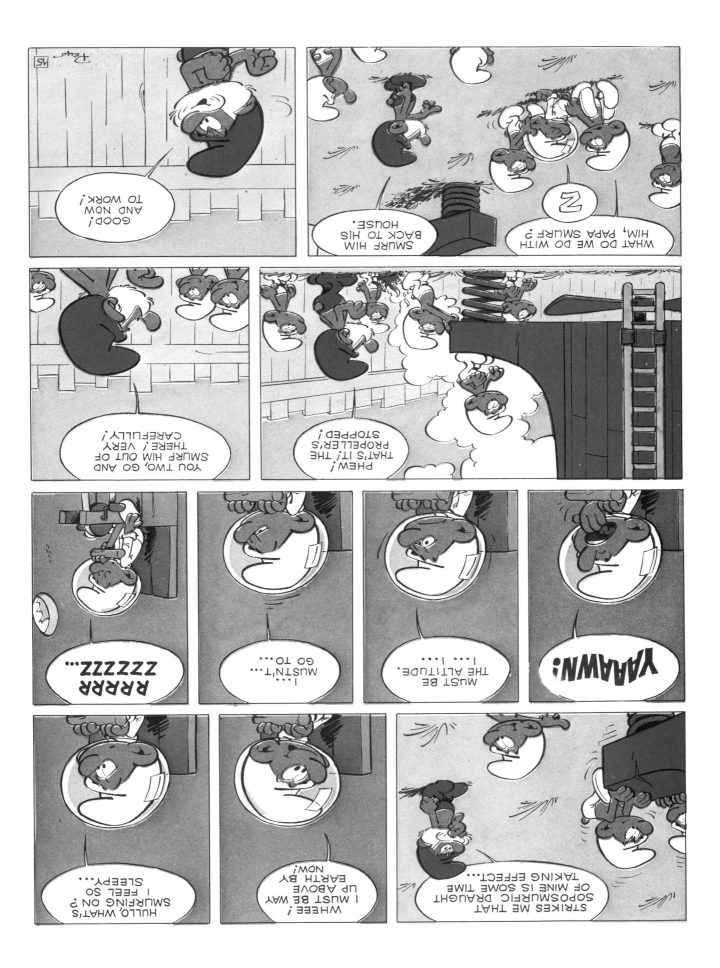

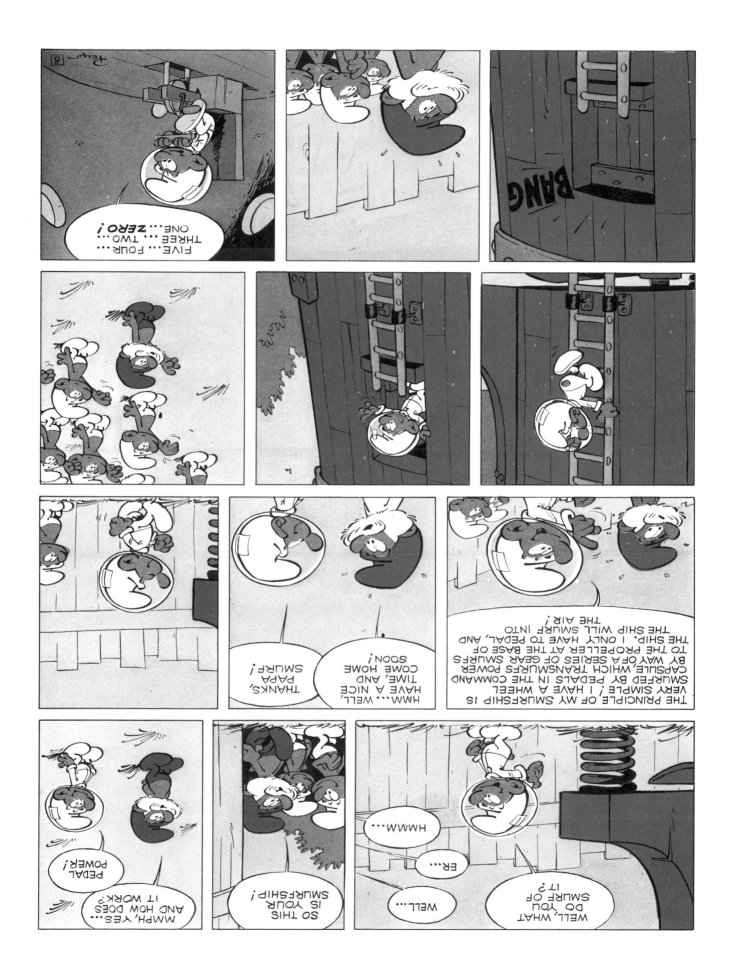

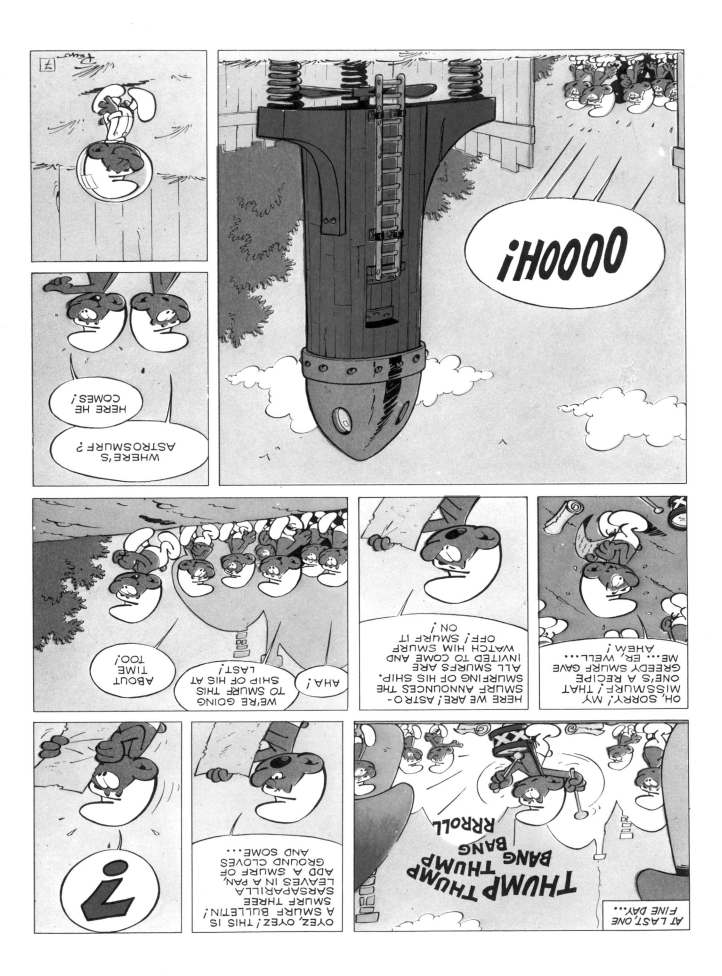

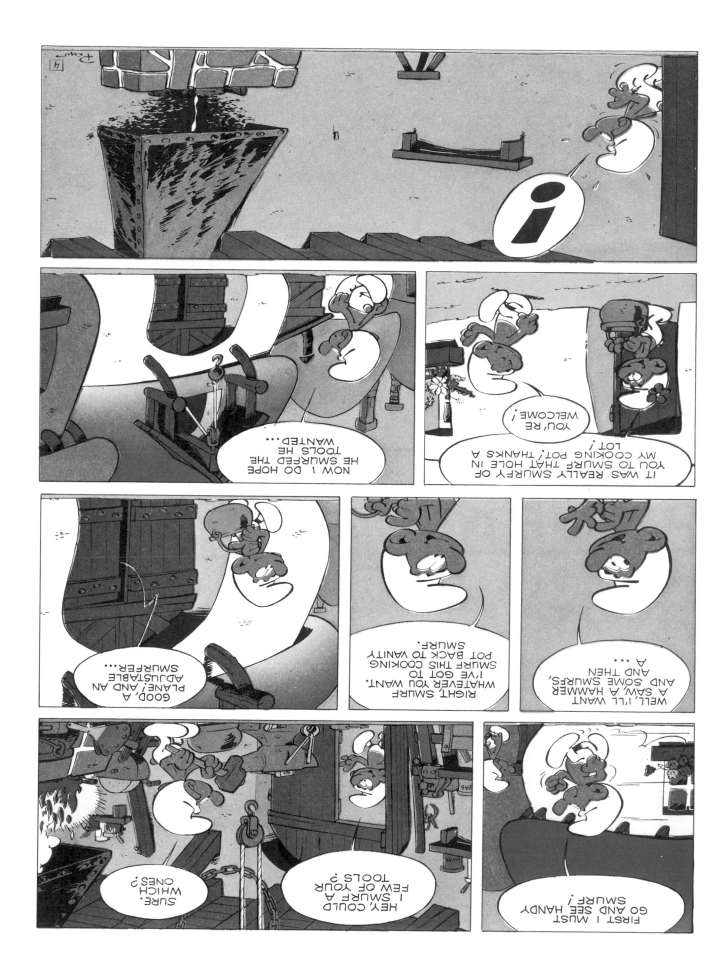

Peyo

a SMURF adventure

The Astrosmurf

Written by DELPORTE and PEYO

Translated by Anthea Bell and Derek Hockridge

Random House 🏠 **New York**

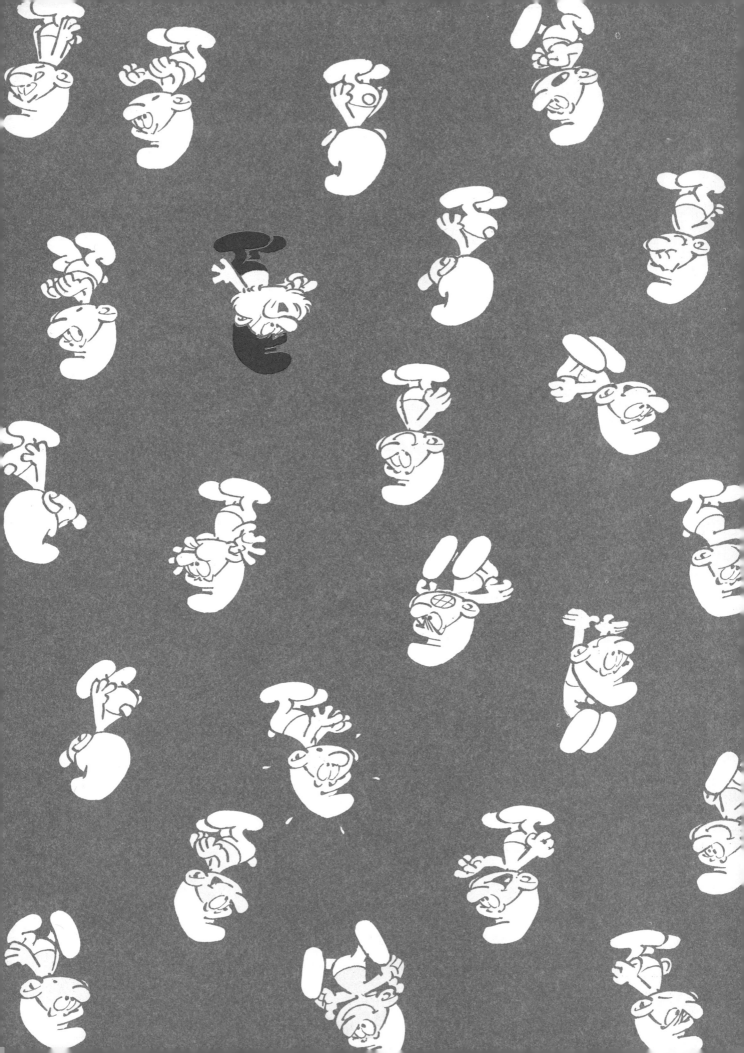